The Inconvenience of You

Jareese Shirlee

Illustrations by Maliyah Scott

DEDICATION

To all those who have been
Inconvenienced.

CONTENTS

INTRODUCTION

This book is a gripping rollercoaster of emotions. The words reflect certain spaces in time I have occupied since I first discovered "Love". My hope is that through sharing where I was, I can help others that have been *Inconvenienced* rediscover self, appreciate their heart, and find the bravery to keep searching for the perfect love. I journaled and prayed to be brave enough to send my heart out into the universe in written form. My only wish was for something beautiful to come back to me.

These words were authored along my journey of self-discovery. There was a point as I travelled through the nuances of love and relationships where I thought I lost me, and I had to find her again. Poetry nurtured that and was (is) my therapy. Love was not the only thing that contributed to the growth in my womanhood, heart break developed me as well. I still believe that love is one of the most important elements of our lives. I finished this book two years ago, I just never felt like it was complete. But it is, and here I present to you in its glory, the words of my heart, the emotions of my past, and the freedom writing this book has brought me.

Thank you for sharing in my journey.

With Love,

Jareese

EVERY TIME...

Every time I open myself to love,
I allow the strings of the harp
        That is my bleeding heart
To learn a new melody
An orchestral version
Of love...
        So heavenly...
Every time...
I hear it.
I see it.
It's advancing towards me.
I know it will destroy me.
So afraid to let the music take over...
        I remember...
But still I begin to play,
Every time.
Every time, I try.
I get braver every day.
I smile at him.
I prepare for him,
Don perfume...
Coif my hair...
It brings me pleasure, such things...
I get better at the strings.
I reluctantly begin to play,
I pluck, pluck, pluck away
I begin to learn the melody,
And every time
        it frightens me.
How amazing it is,
To let myself go,
To wrap myself in the melody

To pluck the strings endlessly
With reckless abandon,
Because I've memorized the cadence.
I know the music now
He finally got me.
            Got me thinking this is destiny.

But yet…
There soon comes the change.
A different arrangement…
One I do not know.

The tempo increases,
The volume crescendos,
The strings snap one by one.
Every time,
        In the end
                I'm drug
                I'm hung
                I'm stung

                I'm left
                Bereft
                My shattered heart swept

Away,
                Without care.
So much I give
So much they take
And I lay awake
Every time
Out of my mind.

Internalizing pain
Enduring the shame…
When I'm making this music,
But he's playing games.
It's always the same.
It's just another time
      Another time I was fooled
      Another time I tried
      Another time I cried

      I swear this happens
      Every time.

The tempo increases, The volume crescendos,

The strings snap one by one

LOVELESS: A CONVERSATION

All you ever did was take from me.

You took my youth,
You took my smile,
You took my love,
And then you left me.

You left me a mess.

You left me with baggage that would take me years to process.
You never poured into me,
I'm still healing from the torment you provided, so readily.

It still baffles me...
Truthfully...
It's been years!
So many tears...
I'm still wrestling with the way in which, ever so slowly
You squeezed the life from me.
Grabbed my spirit,
With the strength of a thousand men...
Got me never wanting to love ever again.
Slowly...
You choked the life from me,
Doing it all with a grin.
You didn't see it as sin,
You just wanted to win.
You were proud of the work you did, the work you put in.
I could see it so clear and hear it in your voice.
This was all your choice.

I believe you truly hate me,
The way you thrived off the pain you gave me!
It gave you power, didn't it?

And my dignity left me.

You squeezed the life from me. Grabbed my spirit,

With the strength of a thousand men...

HOW DO I KNOW?

How do I know when it's over?
How do I know when we're through?
How do I know when the time has come
For me to get rid of you.

How can I tell it's the end?
How can I tell you're not mine?
How can I tell the difference,
Between love and a waste of time?

How can I tell you're not him?
How do I know when to quit?
How do I know
That you'll never grow

How do I know this is it?

-THE END

How can I tell the difference,
Between love and a waste of time?

EVERY MOMENT

Every Moment
As we lay
To God I pray
Like this we'll stay.

Every Moment
I will try
To never pry
To never cry.

Every moment
I'll be worth it
I'll be perfect.

How couldn't you love me?

Every moment
Apologizing…
'Cuz if I got upset,
You'd call it catastrophizing,
You, a master at deflection,
Every moment,
You'd change direction.

So easy for you to flip on
me Got me
Tip toeing
In my own home
So as not to upset you.
God forbid I upset you.

So, I sat

Every moment,
Your docile creature
Waiting to be featured,

As your main lady...
That sh*t sounds crazy.
Look at me!
I let you be free, then
You break away from me?
Every moment filled with effort
Every moment I labored
Every moment I begged
Every moment I spent waiting for you to get it right.
Every late night,
Waiting for you
To wake up and see me,
Still here
Still reaching
Still pushing
Still grabbing
Still clawing
Still tearing
Still ripping
Still shredding
        Fighting
        Because I spent
        Every moment.
And with each moment
I'll lose myself
But I won't see that I've
        Lost me...
I won't realize that
Every moment gone to waste
Every moment led astray
Every moment my heart screams
Will end without you
And leave me with broken dreams

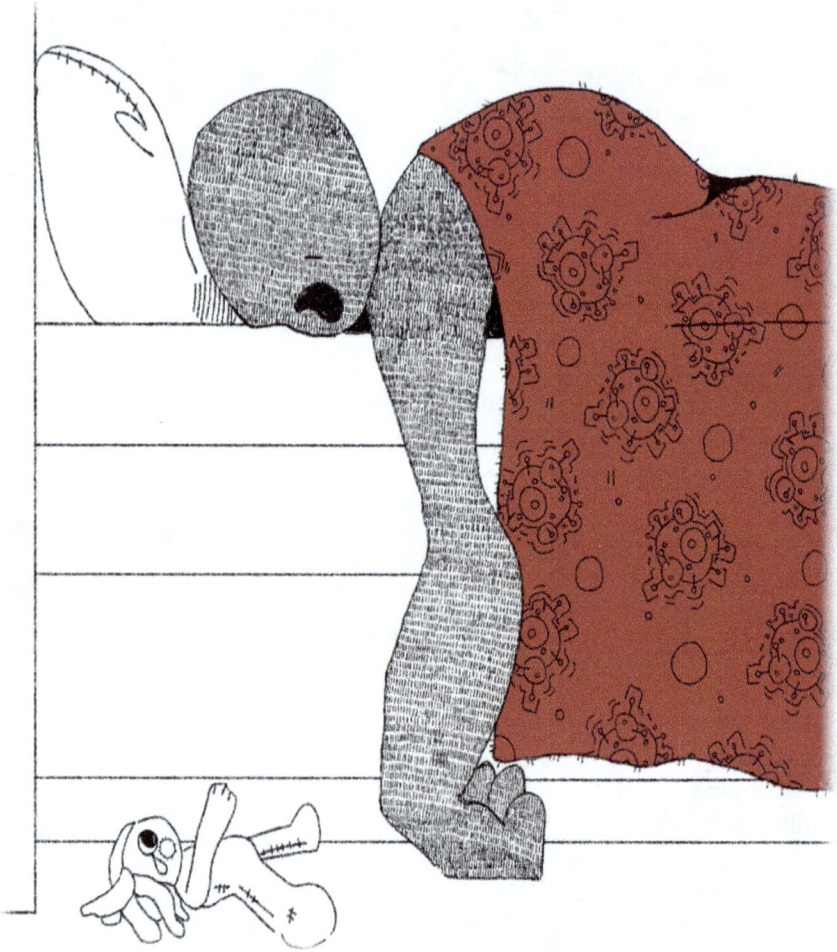

Waiting for you to wake up and see me.

SELF-SABOTAGE

Honestly...

I've never been loved properly.
Only treated like his property
So, when I met you I was terrified.
You knew exactly what you wanted,
And what you wanted was me.

Mind drifts, as I compare
You to the man I'm still in love with.

You asked me, so sweet,
Where did my mind wander off to?
To be honest... do I dare?
No... it's not fair of me
To possess the audacity
To still be in love with him.
He was no good
But God
You....?
You amaze me.
So, trust me...
When I say you don't want me
Believe me!
I am damaged goods
And I am not ready for you.
Because of him!
He was my first everything
To be honest, my future, present, past
And he always comes back...
And I take him, with no questions asked.
So I don't deserve you,
Because I only know him and the way he loves me.
As TRASH as I know that love to be.

I can't accept this gift of
Beautiful you,
Begging to love me.

Wanting to be the man I need
Just trying to save me from me
And we all need a shining knight,
Right?
But to be honest...

My God, I swear...
If I had wings I would fly,
I'd get you outta my hair,
Away I would tear
And run back to that miserable life.

And being quite honest,
You possess every single
Quality and characteristic
Any woman could ever want and need.

And ungrateful,
The mess, silly old me...
Would have the nerve to plead:

GOD!
Why couldn't he be you?

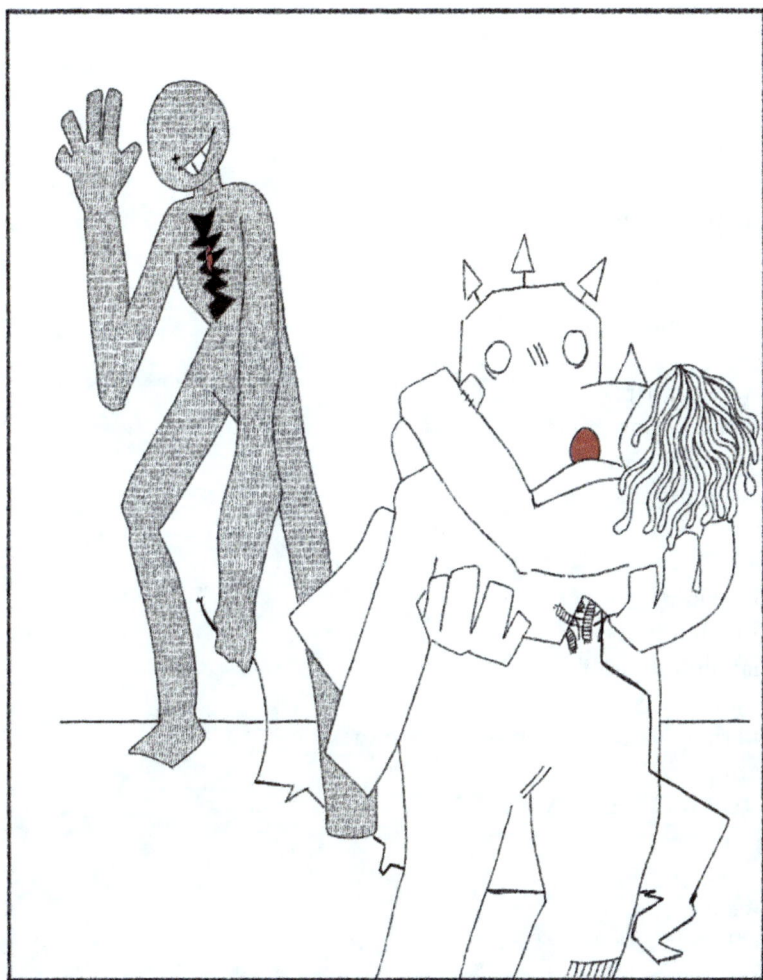

And we all need a shining knight, right?

LOVE AIN'T

I don't know a lot
But I know what love ain't
It damn sure ain't
This constant state
Of chaos.

It damn sure ain't
Worrying and wondering
Real
Or illusion.

Love ain't lists of
Pros and cons
Pondering if the good
Outweighs the bad.
Man… what is that?

Love ain't
Convincing myself.
That ain't my job!
How crazy is that?
Cuz there's no way you don't love me!
Right?
YOU GOTTA LOVE ME?
Right?

Love ain't pain!
But I've loved
And they've harmed me.
Physically.
Emotionally. Mentally.
It's draining me!

Love ain't games!
Ya'll gotta stop playing with me.
Literally and Figuratively,
Hold your sweet words
I know you ain't here for me!

Love ain't waiting!
For a man to decide
Love is not indecisive
Love doesn't waste time.

Love ain't bargaining,
With your soul and your mind.
Love ain't!
Love ain't I GIVE and YOU TAKE!

Love ain't simple
Love ain't easy
Love ain't complacent
And love ain't loving me!

And here I am,
A ball of confusion
Jagged pieces that don't connect
No way of mending it
Love ain't it..
And I'm over it…

I'm just trying to find out what LOVE IS.

I'm just trying to find out what love is...

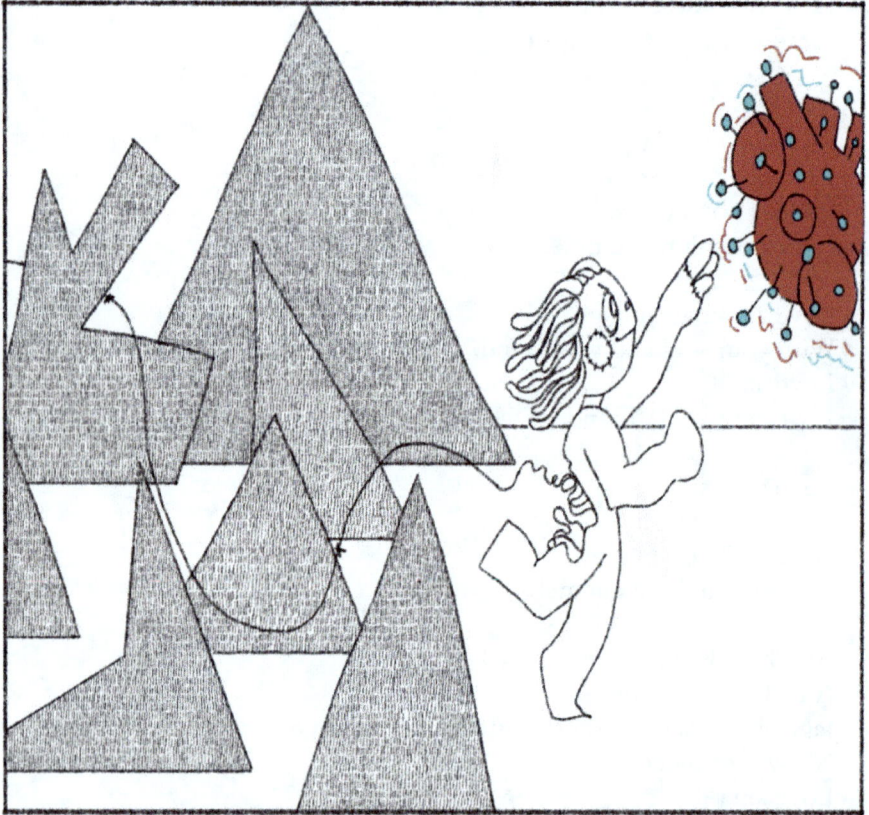

Confusion.

VISION

A weight lifted from my shoulders
To be rid of you at last!
Finally finding all the strength I need
To leave my past in the past.

You do not deserve me now,
But I was scared to shut the door.
But thinking back, I see so clear
What I did not see before.

As a man, you are cut
From the toughest cloth there is
And that is a sensation that
I know I'll never miss.

So goodbye to you
And the cruel games you played
If I never hear your voice
Or see you
I won't be dismayed…
I'll thank God I prayed.

So goodbye to you, and the cruel games you played.

ILLUSION

I refuse to waste
Precious energy
On being angry.
All that you are to me
All you became to me
I allowed you to be.

Now it is hard
To come to terms with your misuse
Of my love and my heart
Your consistent abuse.

I'm disgusted,
And I think "the nerve!"-
It's ME he's using
And I'm disappointed
Because I was fooled
And believed the illusion.

I was fooled and believed the Illusion.

UNCONSCIOUS

I lay unconscious
But I dream about us
I dream of our love
But I know of our lust

This unconscious yearning
Lights my soul on fire
As yet
I am drawn to you
With a force- so magnetic
Like a moth to a flame
I burn with shame-
I cannot shake you
I can't pull away
I struggle and fight
But I'm still drawn to the flame

Wrapping my legs around your waist
As I scream out your name
Fighting back tears because
I let myself lay
Here with you again

Unconsciously

I'm pulled in
And flat on my back
Biting my lower lip

Unconsciously

The lust in your heart
Screws over my soul
Because I love you more
Thank you will ever know

Unconsciousness

That's what led me.

Not caring…
I assumed you met me
Toe to Toe
The feelings I have
I thought you showed
So, in giving myself to you …
to hold…
I got caught in a trap
And I can't let go.

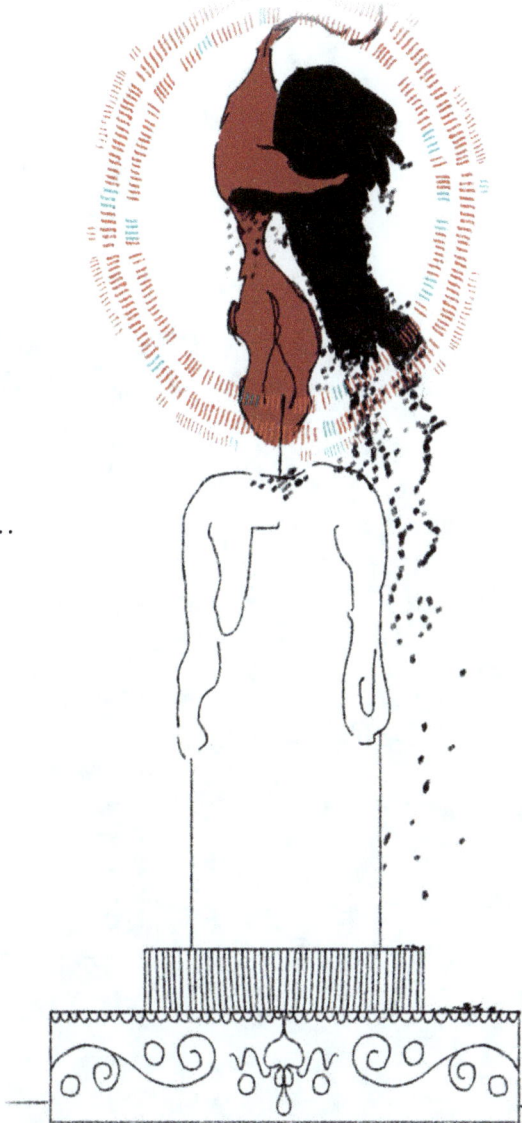

Truth.

INSECURE

I couldn't believe the truth when I began to see
Narcissistic ways laced with misogyny
Sadistic, sad, and sarcastic
Egomaniacal and egotistic
Clearly the fable shines, I see you now
Unattractive and unstable, I
Regrettably am realizing that this
Equals who you are
An insecure, weak-minded individual.

TO WAKE UP TO YOU

As I awake
I reach out for you
But I know you won't be there.
How I wish that you
Would realize
The way in which I care.

You live in my heart
Take space in my head
As the memories replay.
I clench my fists
I wish and wish
And pray you feel the same.

That somewhere out
Among the stars
You lay and you believe,
That I am lying in your arms
And you could wake up to me.

That somewhere out among the stars, you lay and you
Believe...

IF YOU HAVE THE CHANCE TO LOVE

With the pride of a lion
With the heart of a bear
I will love ferociously
I will love without care.

I will fight like a tiger
I will soar like a bird
I will love with great honor
I will love beyond words.

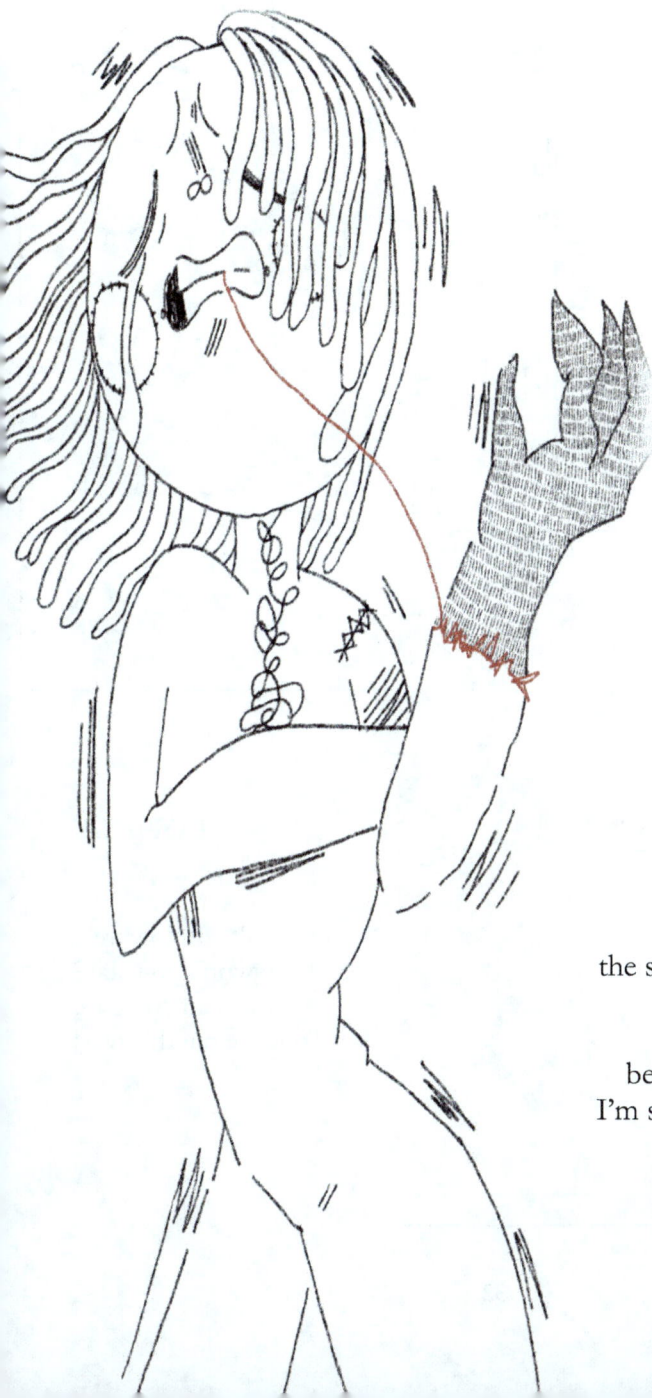

LIES

I can say
I do not love you
I can say
I do not care
I can ignore
your existence
Though I know
you are there.

I can be
fake and friendly
And act like
It's all okay
I can nod,
I can smile
And wish you
Good day.

But LIES.

I'm lying
to accept
the separation of us two.

I am lying
because unfortunately,
I'm still in love with you.

SILLY

I've been crucified for
loving you
But that's none
of your concern
Your all-consuming
Selfish heart
Has left me
to bear that burden.

LONELY

Why won't you love me!
Why won't you stay?
How can you dare
To leave me this way!

TIME FOR LOVE

I stare off in the distance and I daydream and think
I would love to find my soul mate
Truth is I am tired
And I think it's too late

Release.

LET GO

Can't you let go of me,
So I don't have to do it?
I can't let go of you…
I can't put myself through it.

Our time is done!
The time has come!
It's time for us to say goodbye.
Why?

We must release… Let go of me
Let me fall… stop grasping for me,
Stop pulling on me.

I can't hold on,
So why do you?

JUST LET GO.

THE INCONVENIENCE OF YOU

1 I never did imagine
In you, I didn't see.
All the things that I see now,
The things that cannot be.

2 It feels so right to be in your arms,
But the timing is all wrong.
I hate to admit the truth,
But to me you don't belong.

3 And even though the emotions
Are evident in your gaze
The inconvenience of you has
My gentle heart ablaze.

4 It happened so expediently,
In the blink of an eye…
The way in which I fell for you,
But WE are a lie…

5 You cannot be mine…
And I cannot be yours,
But I have already let you in,
And shut and locked the doors.

6 So how can I untangle
The feelings that I feel?
How does one just run away
From something that's this real?

7 I know that you care!
I know you speak true!
Is a leap of faith out of question
Between me and you?

8 Can we bravely leave our
comfort zone,
And begin something new?
With just a hunch how good
It is, when it's just me and you?
The timing is all wrong, so
Whatever shall we do?
Wait around with longing hearts
Until they break in two?

9 So we should sit, and watch,
and wait,
You with her and me with him…
Until the stars reveal our fate
But will we win even then?

10 This is so inconvenient…
The meeting of us two.
Because we cannot be together,
So whatever shall we do?

The Inconvenience of You...

PAST THE ANGER TO A BALL OF CONFUSION

It's always in the back of this mind
The images of you.
I can't suspend it, no matter how I try…
Because I do try,
And I try.

And when I do
Forget about you,
You decide to come around.
It doesn't matter about my life,
Or any new love I've found.

Will you not leave me alone?
Stop calling my phone!
Been disappointed so many times,
I am not mad nor surprised.

I do not know how to be angry at your actions,
I just keep running back.
And you always come back to me,
And I take you like a dummy.

Don't even ask questions about why you left,
I only open my arms and accept.
I let you back in
To cause chaos again.

I don't want you to come back this time,
But I speak that every time.
I want you to leave me alone…
But you know, and I know,
When you call this phone,
I will answer.

When you ask me to come,
I am coming.
When you kiss me and say it's me,
I allow it to be.
I fall into bliss, for a month or two
Then again, with a kiss,
You disappear, and I'm blue.
I know you cannot care about me,
But you comment my beauty…
You make me believe
That I am for you.
You make me believe
This time it is true.

Then I find a picture
Or I hear a story
With you as the star, but yet
I don't play your starlet.
Once again, sad and ashamed.
I hang my head and back away
Into the shadows, and out
Of your sight
Until two months from now
You'll call in the night.

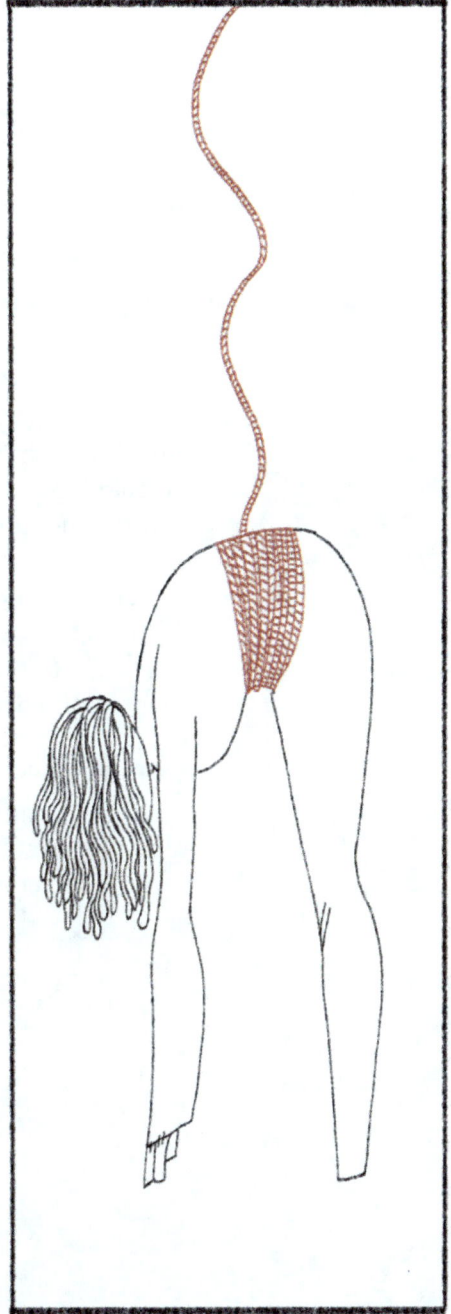

Jareese Shirlee

UNFORTUNATE CIRCUMSTANCES

Completely, I loved you
And I thought you felt the same.
I would jump, and I would shiver
At the mention of your name.

But here I sit, looking dumb as hell,
Feeling foolish as well…
You opened my heart
Then commenced ripping it apart.

Unfortunately, for the life of me
I cannot see,
Why I let circumstances with you
Take control of me.

Unfortunate Circumstances

EVERY ROSE HAS ITS THORN

Everyone watches
While others mourn.

Somebody waits…

Someone else has sworn,
And cursed the stars
For the day he was born.

I ache in turmoil
Alone and forlorn.

Ripping my flesh.
From the bone
It was torn…

In secrecy I ponder
At the bond that was formed.

I partake in the beauty,
Forbidden-
but forewarned…

Each rose so beautiful
Still has its thorn.

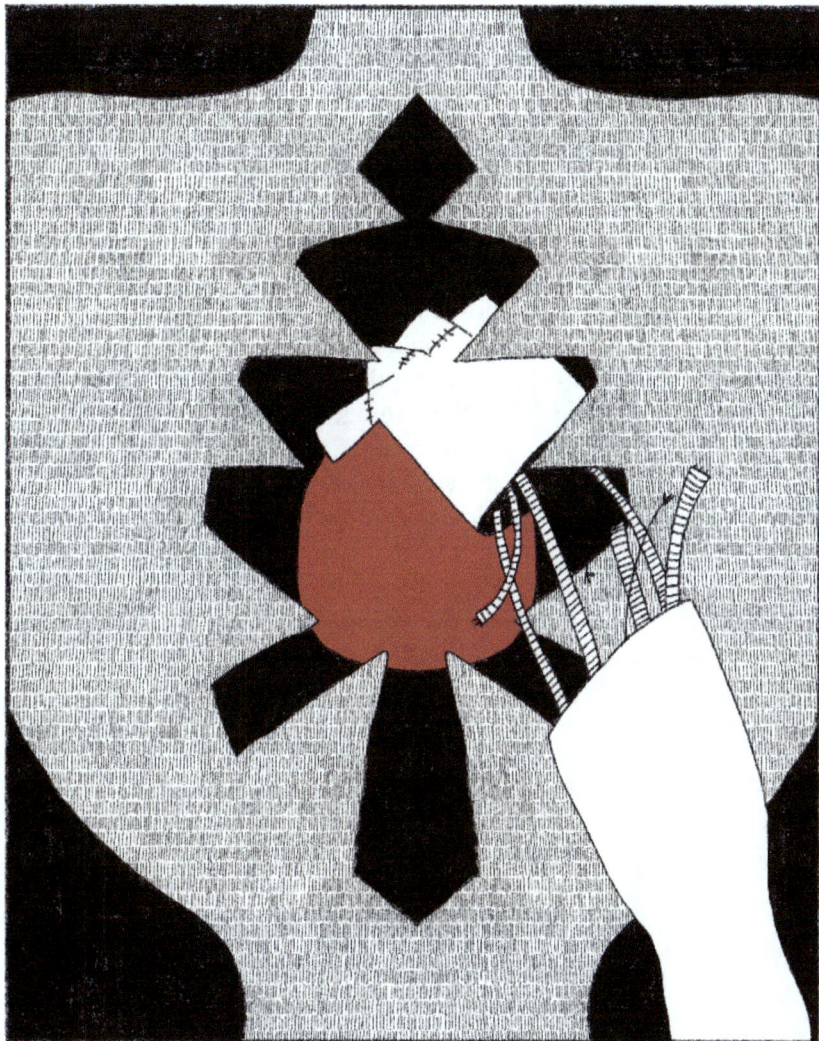

Ripping my flesh, from the bone it was torn...

Jareese Shirlee

RESISTANCE

Someone
Please
SHOW ME
How to put up a fight.
Why does something so wrong,
Feel so right?
Drawn to this man
Knowing it's insane,
And now I am wondering
Who should I blame?
For wanting this to be
Something
it could
Never ever be-
Him and me...
And now I see...
Never together
will we be.
I don't think,
I just move...
I don't run away,
I run to
And now I want him even more
To hold
To kiss
To be all mine...
But with tears in my eyes,
I see it's not time...

I'M SCARED

Let's take it slow.
Let's just see where we go.
This is how it always begins,
Yes, I know.

But I'm scared

I'm scared to completely trust you...
Though I want so much to.

But I'm scared

My heart wants so hard to try,
But by my mind, my heart's defied.

I'm scared

Scared, cuz when we are together
I want to be here forever
And it's soon.

I'm scared.

Scared that I don't really have you.

I'm Scared...

BETRAYAL. PAIN. UNCERTAINTY

My heart sunk down,
To the tips of my toes,
At the thought of you betraying me.

Heart beating fast,
Sweating so cold, sick
At the thought of you betraying me.

Thoughts spinning through my mind,
      Nonstop, over and around.
      Betrayal. Pain. Uncertainty.
      Spirit upside down.

      The depths of my despair,
      No way you can tell.
      No way can I hide it.

I'm left lost and so alone,
Loyalty dead,
Trust gone.

Thoughts
spinning
through
my
mind,

Nonstop,
over and
around.

STOLEN

I no longer desire
To love you,
      Or you,
           Or you.
My will to love
Has been tainted
By continuous abuse.
My will to love has been crushed
By your deception and your lies
My will to love has been stolen
While I cry, my heart does die.

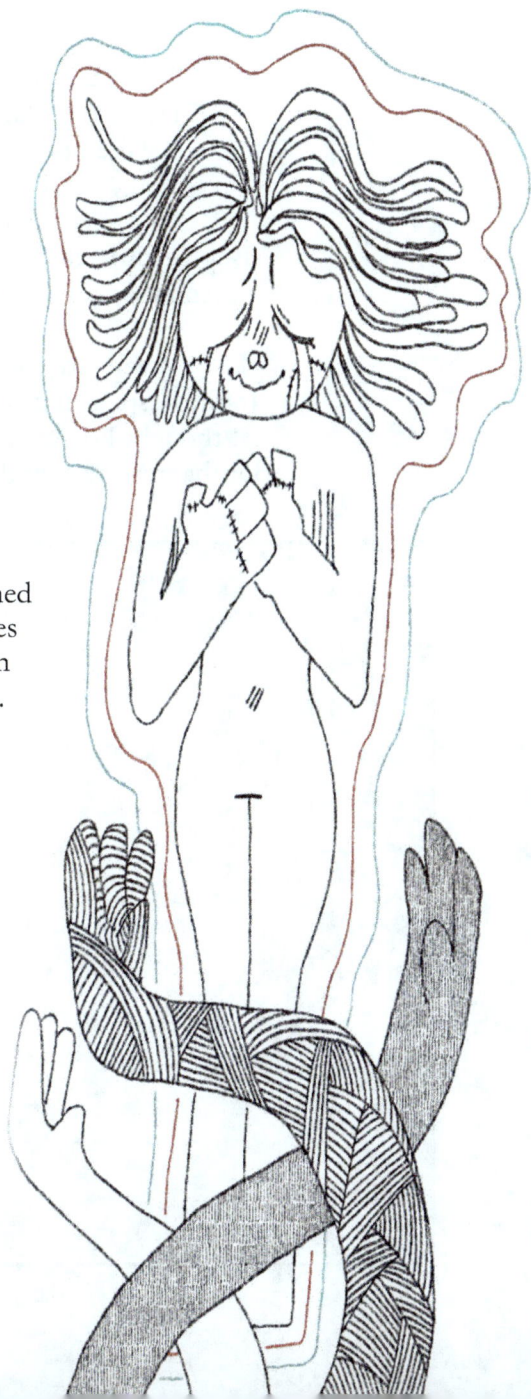

NEVER CAN SAY GOODBYE

Never can say goodbye
But at this time, I must
I treated you like treasure
When you were nothing more than dust
I thought it would be hard
To sever all the ties
But the procedure was too simple
And it seized me by surprise.

I will tarry no longer
In the despair that is your presence
I thought I'd never say goodbye
But that was past, and this is present.

DIGNITY

The unsettled spirit
Is heightened intuition
Never ignore that voice
Take your time and listen

SELF-WORTH

I just want to be seen
Seen for who and what I am.
I want someone to cherish me,
And share with me their plan.
I want someone to look at me and realize.
That I am worth boundless love
And that I am the prize.

I need to be protected,
Like a fragile baby bird…
I need someone to know my thoughts
When I do not speak a word.

And when I am broken
I need someone to lift me up
Kiss my brow, rub my hair
And wrench me from the muck.

My God, I cry out to you!!!
Who can be there for me?!
Then He reached down
Straightened my crown
And said:

"Daughter, YOU can be!"

And then He reached down, and straightened my crown

TRUST LOST

I should just speak-
But I'm not sure.
What makes me weak?
Does it take more strength
To confront what you've done?
Or keep quiet at length?
When I start to build trust,
Unbind these chains
Caked with rust,
Something always happens
To make me change.
Something always happens
To bring me all the pain.
I want someone to protect me
At any and every cost
But not you anymore.

In you, trust is LOST.

REALITY

That painful moment when you realize
Your love is unfaithful-
But is it a surprise?
I love him so
It's only him I see
But if he's unfaithful
How can he love me?
So should I stay
Or should I go?
I'm not sure
I'll ever know.
One thing I'm sure of
As clear as can be
This knowledge has brought me
Spiraling
Back down to reality.

BEAUTIFUL MORNING

Every Morning I wake up to you
Is a beautiful one
Whether the weather is bright with sun
Or the rain beats
like a steady drum
Every morning we share
Wrapped up in each other
Makes me hunger for more
Greedy for another
I open my eyes
So surprised to find
This picture of perfection
That is all mine.

What a beautiful morning.

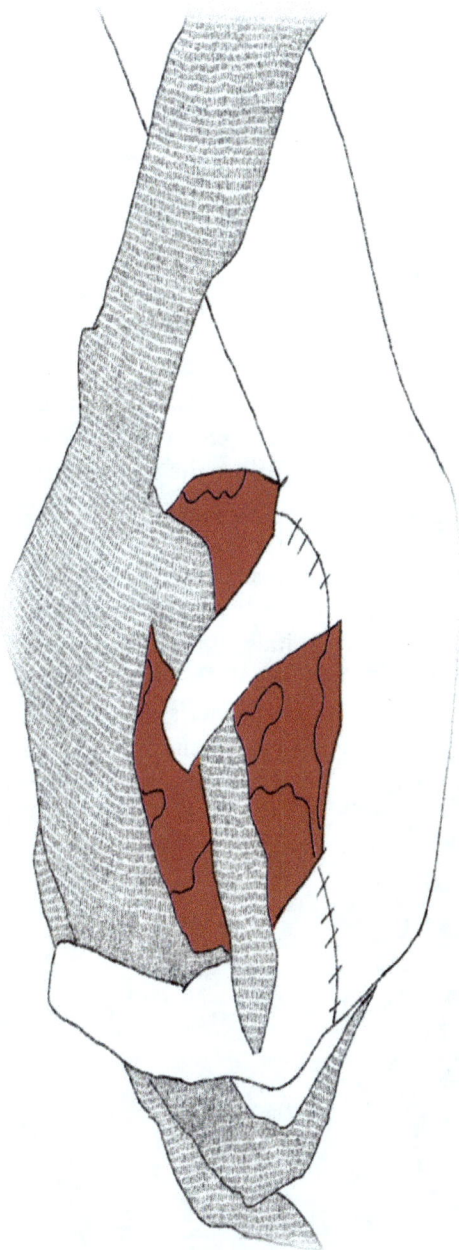

SATISFACTION GUARANTEED

Satisfaction Guaranteed
I will give you
what you need
All you have
to do is ask
Taking control
is no task
Let me be what
you want to have
Let's rule the world,
hand in hand.

THE LIGHT

Look to the light
Reach for the light
It's white and it's bright
Within reach and sight
Will discontinue your plight
Send your life into flight
God's bright light
Shines all through the night
With all of His might
Our Father's never contrite
Just believe in His light
And your life, heart, soul
Will be right.

THE DARK

The oceans,
Deep with unmoving waters
Like a soul full of the blackness of despair
The sorrow of the moon light
As it hovers in the air.

Blood gushing from a wounded heart,
Not a self-inflicted wound
But maybe it is...
Maybe it was...
The answer won't come too soon.

Can you see me up here?
Amidst the clouds and the trees
I'm floating up with no fear
With my tears on the breeze.

In the dark, in the rain
That's seeping through my skin
I'm so aware of the pain
That is steadily sinking in

Something like that color, bright
Crimson, like a rose...
Or black as night,
My unending carousel, my foes.

The color of my anger; red
My hatred an inky hue
Life's not good, rather be dead
Have the world forget me too.

RIGHT AND LEFT

In my right hand
I hold this pen
Mind dictates what is RIGHT

In my left hand
I hold the remnants of
What is LEFT of my life

LEFT is trying, praying, struggling
To get on track with

What is RIGHT.

The RIGHT is righting
Oblivious to what is or may become
LEFT or RIGHT

RIGHT is right
And never wrong
So I RIGHT, and RIGHT, and RIGHT

LEFT in touch with reality
Trying to grasp at what is RIGHT

LEFT in touch with all the wrongs
Committed in my life

I'm picking up the pieces
Sorting through this

LEFT
and
RIGHT.

Right...

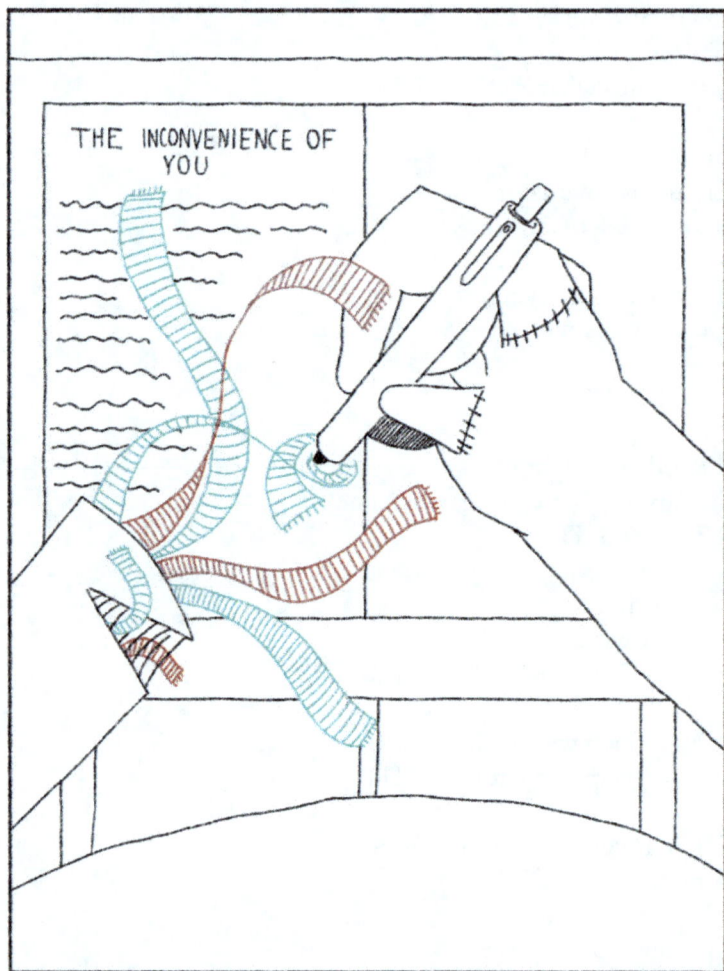

Left....

RIGHT still
Righting
Righting
Righting

Not a thought of LEFT
or
RIGHT

While the LEFT
Does all the thinking

Sorting through what's left of right.

Right?

Am I RIGHT...
Or RIGHT of what is left?

What can be LEFT

Of RIGHT
When we never know what's LEFT

RIGHT IS LEFT
LEFT IS RIGHT
NEITHER RIGHT NOR LEFT IS
WRONG
OR RIGHT...
LEFT.

Remember.
Rise.
Recall.
Fall.

CLOSE YOUR EYES

I close my eyes
And say a prayer
So when I open them
You'll be there

I close my eyes
And make a wish
And purse my lips
To blow your kiss

Tell me your secrets
Tell me your dreams
Don't be afraid to
Fall in Love with me

Now close your eyes
And make a wish
And take a leap

Of faith
On this.

Reminisce.

Be my dream, not
my nightmare.

Jareese Shirlee

INFATUATION

The hair on your head
Your caramel-colored skin
The arch of your eyebrows
The shape of your eyes
The length of your eyelashes
The two moles on your nose
The sexiness of your lips
The straightness of your teeth
The broadness of your chin
Your eyes
Your neck
The curvature of your back
I trace the moles there
The strength of your arms
Your hands, the perfect size
The softness of your fingertips
Electricity in your touch
The length of your nails
Your well-defined chest
Each muscle of your stomach
My hands caress
Fingertips to your firmness
Strong, thick thighs
Smooth brown knees
Calves round and taut
Your ankles, perfection
Even your ankles send me chills
The fact that I know every inch
Of the canvas God created
Will lead anyone to conclude that:

I'm past the point of admiration, lookin' into your chocolate-colored eyes, I know this is infatuation

Jareese Shirlee

I'M PAST THE POINT OF ADMIRATION.
Lookin' into your chocolate-colored eyes
I know this is infatuation
When I'm to the point where
A mere glance at you
Sends fireworks coursing through my body,
Avalanches to occur
The sun and moon to move
Stars to explode
You make me quiver
When hearing your voice
Sends electric currents down my back
Shocks me with shivers
The sky to fall
And the clouds to rain on me
I'm past the point of admiration
I know this is infatuation.
Yeah, yeah, *I'm past the point of admiration.*

I know…

THIS IS INFATUATION.

YOUR EYES SAVED ME

Deep Pools of Chocolate Syrup
Glaze the surface of my brain
As I gaze into your eyes

You can read my thoughts
You chase my soul from hiding
To my surprise

With my heart on my sleeve
You enrapture my spirit
Through your eyes; I see.
Through your ears; I hear it.

Your speech a wafting melody
Calling me from this place.
Pulling me… earthbound from space

Twinkling stars smile down Through
swirling mists as I descend.

I land effortlessly beside you
With the comfort in knowing
This beginning is my end.

YOU DON'T MATTER ANYMORE

You Don't Matter Anymore-
Like a leftover paper plate
Or a Styrofoam cup
Candy wrappers
And soda cans
A brown paper bag or
Last week's newspaper...
You don't matter anymore.

You Don't Matter Anymore-
Like a graded paper or
A lost sock
Too small shoes
And broken toys
A Christmas sweater in the summertime
or Shorts in the winter...
You don't matter anymore.

You Don't Matter Anymore-
Like last week's zit
An old toothbrush
A stray dog
And a faded scar,
The way I used to wish on stars
Or broken cars...
You don't matter anymore.

You Don't Matter Anymore-
Like how you didn't think of
My feelings or
How you used to hurt me.

The way you were loved
And my ripped-up heart
Your tears in the rain
And my old pain
You don't matter anymore.

You Don't Matter Anymore...

MUCH MORE THAN THIS

I am so much more
Worth so much more
Need so much more
Than this.
I am more than the way
You make me feel
More than your love-
          Less kiss.
I am more than the lies
You always tell
More than abuse
That is mental
I am much more than
This emotionless furor
You give me-
          As a test.
I am much more than this Waste
you pile on me.
I'd rather be lonely
Than this.
I am so much more
Than the pain
You leave me with
Time after time.
I am much more than
The hurt
I'm left to heal
Saying "I'll be fine".
I am much more
Than the tears I shed
Because my heart's yours-
But yours isn't mine.

THIS

You are not real,
You are my Dream.
Because in my dreams
You are not mean, and
You love me how
You used to love.
I miss the way
We used to hug-
So look at me
Deep in my eyes
I am no fool,
Please... Recognize.
I know that you
May not be true
But I hope one day
That you mean to
I do not want
To let THIS go
Instead I crave
For this to grow
And as I sit
As I surmise...
I wonder if
You tell me lies
And will you ever
Realize
That THIS is real?
And so time flies...
I do not know
If THIS will last
But Prayerfully
THIS doubt shall pass.

HAPPINESS...?

An endless reverie-
You and me...
Your enchantment is
My melody.
The thought of you

Makes me so happy.
Will you kiss me?
Will you caress my body?
Rub against my thighs,
Undress me with your eyes?
Heart beats so fast
Cares so far cast
Away...

Tumbling back down to reality.
This is only how I want it to be,
This is how it will never be,
For you and me.
To the outside world
It's the way it seems,
But happiness for me
Is only in my dreams.

But happiness for me, is only in my dreams

FLY

I'm gonna FLY
Up so high in the sky
I'll leave behind all this pain
My tears will be rain
Fly up to the clouds
I don't want to come down
Ever again
I don't want to descend
Fly
Fly fly
I'll say goodbye
I'll start a new life
On golden wings
That prayers may bring
Fly to meet my happiness
And put this all to rest

I WONDER... WHY?

Why
I deserve to cry,
Why
I want to die.
Why
You would walk on by?
Why, why, why...

Why
My heart's denied.
Why
I'm vilified.
Why
Do I even try ?
Why, why, why...

But God says
"Why child? Why Cry?
My Son died,
So you can fly.
So wipe your eyes,
Spread your wings up high,
Keep your head to the sky."

FOLLOW ME

What will happen?
What will be?
Between him and me.
I thirst to know him
Intimately,
And kiss his lips
So tenderly.
To hold him and know
He belongs to me.
But so absurd!
Damn my dreams!
Confusion overtakes me,
Inside I scream!
He says don't think,
Just follow me…
The blind fold's on
And I don't dare breathe.
I know not what
He has for me
Nor what place
He's leading me
But because I thirst For
him intimately
I blindly follow
As he takes the lead.

TRUTH

Here it comes, the way I feel
Am I dreaming, or is this real?
Too damn good, to be so true
Sinning should never feel this good…
I feel so guilty for wanting him
Good vs. Bad… Which side will win?
Don't get caught! I preach
But common sense is outside my reach
And sensitivity is within my grasp
But selfishness wins out at last
I may be wrong, but I want him bad
And at myself I remain so mad…
I should do right
And walk away
But I'll probably do wrong and stay.

I DON'T CARE

If you weren't aware
I no longer care.

I don't care about you
Or your hopes, or your dreams
I don't care about you
Nor about any thing

That has to do with you, or
The air that you inhale.
The space you take up is a waste,
I just wish you'd go to hell.

That's not true,
But I take that back,
You mean nothing at all,
I don't care about that.

You laid with her so many times, and
Then came back to me
You endangered my life, my faith, my heart
you caused insanity.

For no known reason
You ruined my trust.
You cared about nothing
other than your own lust.

I was just sport,
Just a conquest you won
Not important, Unloved
Toyed with for fun.

But now here is the issue
Because I don't care at all
I don't care if you stumbled,
I don't care if you fall.

I don't care if you wake up,
I don't care if you come back.
I don't care if you figure out
How a gentleman should act.

I just simply do not care.
Insert a shoulder shrug right here
If it has anything to do with you,
To the left, kind sir, take that over there.

TRUE LOVE

This life I lead
Confuses me…
I have been hurt
So I am afraid to Love…
I am afraid my heart will break
Or continuously be broken…
So my heart I do not open…
But then I run the risk of forgetting what this is
And by this I mean true love
Which I haven't felt in so long.

CAN YOU?

Can you wrap your arms around me?
Be the one to set me free?
Can you calm my troubled spirit,
With a gentle kiss for me?
Can you be my protection,
In the midst of fire and pain?
Can you be my comfort...
And the shelter from the rain.

APPLAUSE

Staring out the window
Wondering what's real
Battling the wounds
Not even time can heal
In anguish for myself
Wondering in confusion
Why do I deserve this?
Bewildered by delusions
Searching for the reason
Grasping at the straws
Gazing in the mirror, and
Numbering my flaws
Clenching up my fists
About to go insane
Jumbled on the inside
Thundering with pain
Re-examining each moment
At each memory, I pause
My tears fall in a torrent
I capture the applause.

Staring out the window
Wondering what's real

NO MORE

No more long-suffering
No pining away
No more begging and pleading
No more saying "Please stay"
Goodbye to you love
What once was is no more
I refuse to fight for this
I will no longer mourn
You can go far away
I will no longer follow
There is nothing left
My heart's become hollow

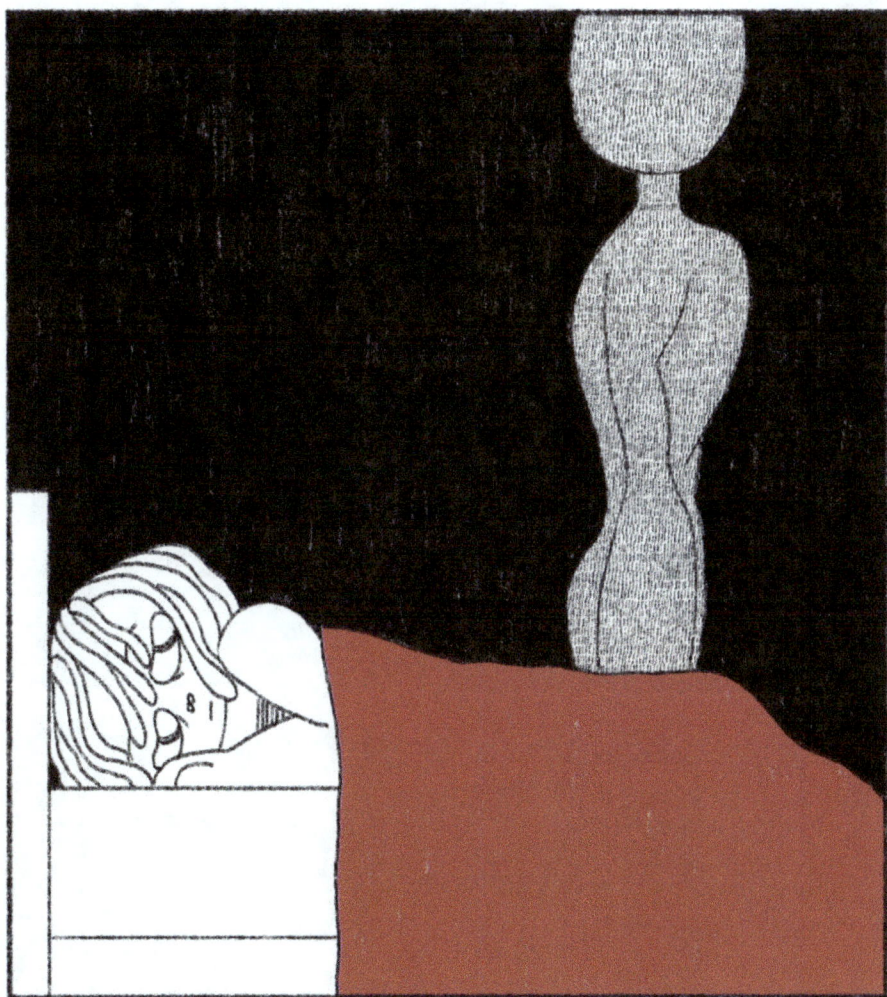

No More

Jareese Shirlee

THE FAULT IN OUR STARS

The fault in our stars
Is they never align
Either you shine
Or I shine
But never at the same time.

The fault in our stars
Is I'm day and you're night
And try as we might
To combine our light
We can never get it right.

The fault in our stars is
We're on different paths
Though we share the same laughs
Memories of times past
And they're fading so fast.

The fault in our stars
Is we are attracted, dangerously
Sure to combust, spontaneously
In love against odds, erroneously
But co-existing, figuratively.

The fault in our stars to be…
Without you with me!
To shine separately
Is an anomaly.

We can find a way together.

The Fault in Our Stars

WORTHY

I don't know how I can keep going
With the knowing
That no one ever loves me
No one ever cares
No one ever.

Here is your out...
I am giving you your out.
I'm setting you free.
You are free to leave and go,
Far away from me.

I can't be left with this pain and I can't
Be forced to accept,
The way you treat my heart
Leaves me twisting in regret.

You can go on.

I'm setting you free
You are free to leave and go

PRIZE

Straighten your crown
And realize
He is the clown
And you are the prize

Peace.

MASK

Never disguise
your truth for lies
In the end
it will be no surprise
You will be the one
everyone side eyes.

Awaken.

RAGE

Incongruent.
Disjointed.
Standing in the mirror.
Eyes Crossing.
Disbelief.
You will never do this to me again.

Re-Center.

LOVE YOURSELF

Love yourself.
Be all you need.
The Power is Yours.
You will succeed.

You are the goal.
You are the dream.
You are the light.
Your words, the seed.

Peace.

Self-Love.

A NEW ME

I will not allow your presence to defeat me.
I cannot give you the courage to unseat me.
I will not provide you the chance to unground me.
I cannot give you the power to uncrown me.
I won't let you laugh when I am referred to as a Queen.
I will not offer you the chance to render me unseen.
I refuse to continue to return the energy you give.
I cannot receive it… I have my best life to live.
I will not allow you to scoff at my self-confidence,
Or diminish all my spiritual gifts, 'cuz God made me like this
I will stop insistent attempts to diminish my beauty.
I will discontinue listening, as you disparage rudely.
This is the end of your torture and your tyranny.
I will take back my control. You don't deserve a Me.

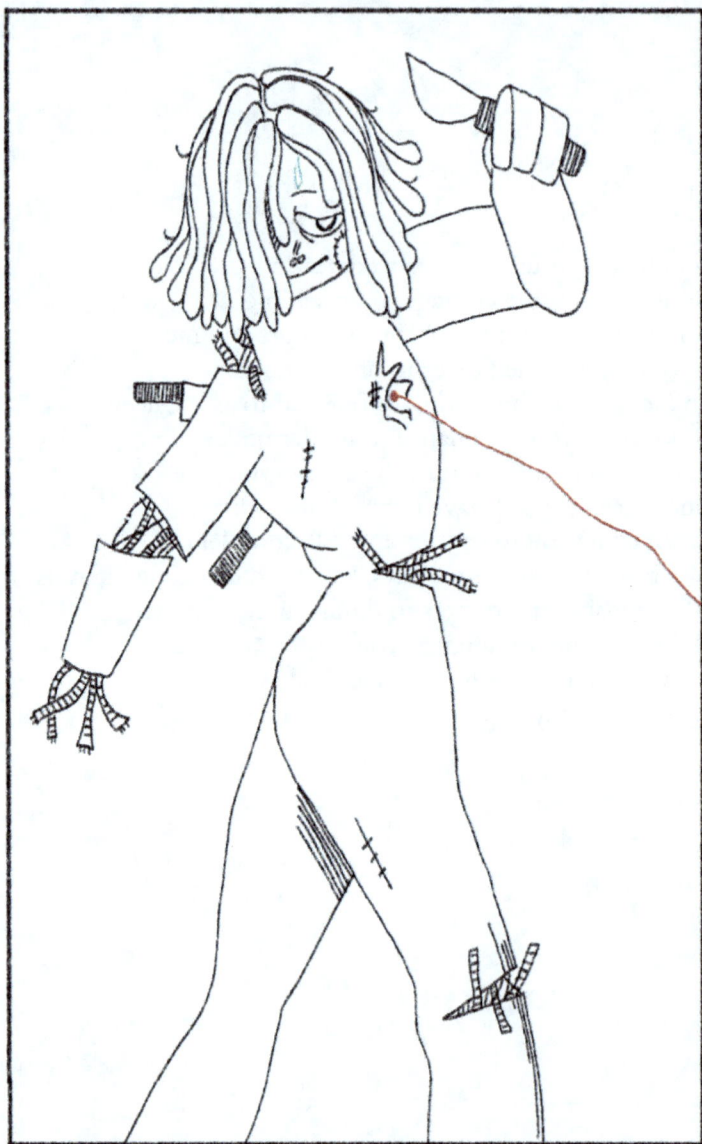

This is the end of your torture and your tyranny

Reflect.

PICTURE ME

Visualize the life you crave
Picture yourself
In the middle of your hopes and dreams
You...
Making your fairytale come true
Rose petals at your feet
The clouds as your pillow
Smell, touch, taste…
Romanticize
The life that you deserve
Deciding, intentionally
What is best for "ME".
Your dreams are your destiny.
So never give up until you create
Your greatest reality.

SUCCESS

Success is only what you
Define it to be
And different for every
Single being.
What's paramount to you
Could be insignificant to some
But that will never diminish
the jewel you will become.

HOLLOW

Inside I'm hollow,
With no way out
And no way to contain.

I'm on a quest,
Searching for a cure
To alleviate this pain.

I'll do anything
I can to try
To feel whole again.

I'll damage, scream,
Kill, and destroy,
And make you feel the same.

If I feel pain,
Then you'll feel pain.
I'll drown you as my tears flow like rain.

Because inside I'm hollow
With no way out
And no way to contain.

I WANT YOU, BOY...

I want you, boy...
I do.
But more than you
I crave my peace.
Baby, I don't want the streets
They ain't for me
I don't belong in
Ratchet-ry
But I won't war for your attention
Baby, no...
Not never, no more
That's not the way
This 'bout to go.
So listen up, I WANT YOU, Boy!
I want your kids
I want to share the holidays
Matter of fact
I want to cater to you in every way
I want to submit
And let you lead
I want to feel safe in your gaze.
But baby,

NOT AT THE EXPENSE OF ME!

And THAT's where we go left.
I need reciprocity,
And not incessant mess.

Heal.

TWO DAYS

What has occurred in two days,
That makes you treat me this way?

Or has it really been two days?
Maybe it has always been this way...
But now my blind eyes
Are open... where is your disguise?
You look identical now as when we first met,
But somehow, oh so different...
You, with that beautiful complexion,
You used to pay so much attention
To me...we loved each other's company
You couldn't keep your hands from me...
Your eyes would never stray...
Never, from me, stray away.
The phone rang endlessly
Conversations... you and me...
You loved to kiss my lips
Rub your hands across my hips
Our bodies fit so well together
But is that feeling gone forever?
You... Please don't go away from me
Please, I don't know why you're leaving me...
What has caused this change?
Caused your heart to rearrange?

What has occurred in two days,
That makes you treat me this way?

WHATEVER HAPPENED TO US?

How could this be?
I'm sitting here in disbelief...
Are you actually leaving me?
Doesn't all this time mean anything?
So now you're leaving, like a summer fling?
You're packing your bags and walking out the door?
You don't want to be here anymore?
I can't believe it's actually true,
You're leaving, and I still love you!
Whatever did I do wrong?
To cause you to leave after this long?
After all the times we fed each other,
The way we cuddled, massaged one another...
Whispering sweet nothings in my ears
Making sure I had no fears...
Comforting me when I cried
I tried to understand it, I tried
I can't believe it 'cuz we've never fussed
So whatever happened to us?
You are causing my life to erupt
You know how much I love you
So how can you say we're through?
You've done all you could do?
I thought I was the one for you...
I can't just say "Forget You."
Cuz, simply, I STILL LOVE YOU...
Tell me please, was this all lust?
Oh God,
Whatever happened to us?

LOVE #1

When you smile,
I cry…
And I wish I
Would die.
Because I know,
This won't last…
And it makes
Me so sad.
Because I love you,
And I need you,
I want you in my life…
I want to be your wife.
You and me…
We could be…
Eternally Happy,
But you are leaving,
You want her,
Instead of me,
How could this be?
Don't I mean anything?
Yes, you've given me honesty
But honestly,
Why have the truth
When the lie is so much better?
Why be… not in truth,
When in lie we are together.
Tell me you love me!!!

Give me a sign!!!
Tell me you want me,
So I know you are mine.
In my heart
I feel this cannot be...
In my mind
I know otherwise.
You must feel
What I feel,
I see it in your eyes!
I am mourning you leaving,
I'll do anything for you to stay.
I wish I had known
It would turn out this way.

GOOD MORNING

Good morning to you, Love.
Your sweet kiss
Upon my lips
As we lie here in down pillows,
The ceiling fan, circling lazily above.

Blowing warm air
Across our bare flesh.
Limbs tangled in an endless
Mass of white sheets,
Intertwined-
Your hands in my hair..

White lilies in a glass vase,
Sunlight streaming through slated blinds
Silly drunk off love's wine
We giggle kissing tenderly-
Forgetting about the time.

Our Love is pure,
Like the morning sun
Though the clock chimes one...
Here we lay, here we stay...

Our Love is beautiful.

HAIKU: Tears In Spring

1.
Your eyes as you cry:
Like the first spring rain at dawn...
Pools of red and water.

2.
As I see the rain
From the spring dew of your eyes
I am drawn to you.

3.
Beautiful stranger
Like my own blooming spring rose
May I come to you?

THIS MORNING I WOKE UP

This morning I woke up
And you weren't by my side...
To you I cannot talk to
To you I can't confide.
I do not like the stolen nights
We share
Because nothing can compare
To the nights we spend carelessly
Wrapped in eternal bliss
In your kiss...
Except the time that we are apart,
And both times devour my heart.
I feel like I know you,
But then again... I don't!
And I want to be a part of you,
But you won't
Give me you... when that's all I ask
Time passes slowly...
The stars ignite, then die...
I am left to slowly wonder:
What do I mean to you?
What can I do?
Do I mean anything?
Am I everything?
Can you tell me you don't burn
With this fire?
That you don't yearn
For me?

YOUR FUTURE, YOUR PAST

If there is a common disconnection
Between our jargon, I'll correct it.
Needing to feel your essence,
Always missing your loving presence.
Forever in your spirituality,
Covered by the comfort you've given me.
You're on my mind, so constantly
Your unique perfection is-
Constantly-
Driving me to need to please you
In any and every endeavor.
Living for the two of us,
I will never breach this trust.
I know this is real, because I'm not afraid
Of the feelings I feel
and the love that we made.
I want this beauty to forever last
To be your future and your past.
This poem I cannot share with you
Because I want this dream to come true.
So I will drown in this reverie
Hoping you'll one day marry me.
A strong emotion
As deep as an ocean
To build our relationship ever higher
Our souls together will never get tired.
As I stare
Down deep
into your soul
into your eyes…
The moment overwhelms me
And I begin to cry
Because of the love
I feel inside.

SANDY SHORES

To be one of two
Is a dream come true!
And here, I am surprised…
The feelings entrenched
Deeper inside me,
Are you telling truths or telling lies?
It's been so long since I've been loved
And everything is new…
And I can't help but
To be afraid
When I think of leaving you.
You say that it's love,
I say so too,
But still afraid I stay…
Will this be ruined as I say goodbye-
As I go away?

Like a beach,
So calm, so warm
And blue with Sandy Shores
My heart can't help but wonder
Should it build walls
And close the doors???
But if I may
With all my might
Wish on a falling star…
I'd make this wish,
I'd dream tonight
You'd remain where you are.

I've worked so hard,
I've toiled so long,
I've given blood and bone
Please, my love,
Oh, please my sweet,

Don't leave me all alone.
Far away, across the miles
Hardened Earth
To Sandy Shores
From every side of the universe
Will you stay mine?
'Cuz I'll stay yours.

REALITY???

You are surreal.
I can't explain what you've given me.
Your touch leaves my soul fuzzy.
You leave me…
Disbelieving… How could a fingertip
Run down my arm…graze my lip…
Have me craving you so bad?
It's so good, just the thought
Is more than enough
To send me over the edge of Reality.
I'm floating, it's true
There's no gravity…
In the realm of me and you.
You have made it possible for me
To be happy.

Jareese Shirlee

SIMPLE LOVE

I found that love will never be
As simple as it seems.
It's never cookie cutter,
Never all rainbows and dreams.
But in simple terms, I'd have to say
That I have come to find
What love means to me
Is choosing growth and compromise,
To choose the player and build the team…
To find the carpenter with the skill
To help you build your dreams.
To find the perfect doctor willing to repair
Your heart at the seams.

TIME TO LET GO....

A sage soul whispered
Unto me
Using a breath of wind
Blew a kiss into
My soul and spoke
Life to me again
Spirit energizing me,
Using chills to
Move throughout.
I sit back,
I just let go
As spirit controls the route.
My heart glows from inside of me as
I discover brand new meaning.
My eyes, they close,
Acknowledging love…
And I begin my healing.

-THE END-

ACKNOWLEDGMENTS

Thank You, God.

Thank you to Maliyah Scott, my illustrator, for undertaking this project with me. Your patience has been paramount. You gave this book the touch I was searching for, and I appreciate you so much. I can't wait until the next go round.

Thank you to Mishunda Mathis, for your love, support, and faith in me during the completion of this project. You gave me the encouragement to complete this work.

Thank you to Xavier Bryant, my childhood friend. As children we wrote together, grew together, and encouraged each other's craft, thinking, and revolutionary ideas. Writing back and forth with you is one of the reasons I can write a poem about any topic under the sun. It was us against the world, so I thank you for being my right hand when we were children.

Thank you, dear reader, for reading this work and coming along this journey with me.

Lastly, thank you.

Thank you, each of you, for the Inconveniences of the past. This has made me who I am today. In some ways without you, this work would not exist. Even indirectly, I can go back to a space in time and recall the emotions I felt and pull from those experiences. So, while this isn't my current reality, it is a part of my evolution. I hope you bear witness to it.

P.S. Don't flatter yourself. I bet you think this poem is about you, don't you? I can promise, it's not. Some of you think more of yourself than you ought to 😊 But you, you know who you are.

ABOUT THE AUTHOR

Jareese Shirlee currently resides in the DMV area. She is a talented writer and has a love for all things literature. Jareese is a loving mother to two sons, Tobias and Cameron, and a puppy-daughter named CoCo Chanel. By day Jareese is an active duty Naval Officer, and by night she is a keyboard warrior chasing her dreams of becoming a published author. Outside of writing, her interests include fashion, dancing, fun experiences, and binge-watching shows in her free time. Her affinity for the written word is sure to shake the world.

Connect with Jareese Shirlee

Instagram: @jareese_shirleewrites
Facebook: @jareese_shirleewrites
TikTok: @jareese_shirleewrites
Email: Jareese.b.shirlee@gmail.com

ABOUT THE ILLUSTRATOR

Maliyah Scott was born in Fort Benning, Georgia and currently resides in Augusta, Georgia. She is a self-taught artist with aspirations of becoming an animator, mostly working in Procreate and Photoshop. She showcases her digital paintings on her Instagram @maliyahsart and her life doodles and comics on Instagram @maliyahsjournal.